Devastated by a VOLCANO!

Disaster SURVIVORS

by Stephen Person

Consultant: Allison L. Payne
Alaska Volcano Observatory
Anchorage, Alaska

BEARPORT
PUBLISHING

New York, New York

Credits

Cover, © Christian Kapteyn/Alamy and Jim Sugar/Corbis; Title Page, © Jim Sugar/Corbis; 4, © SuperStock; 5, © Stephen & Donna O'Meara/Photo Researchers, Inc.; 7T, © Barry Lewis/Corbis; 7B, © Dominique Chomereau-Lamotte/AFP/Getty Images; 8, Courtesy of United States Geological Survey; 9, © Pacific Stock/SuperStock; 10, © Robert Harding Picture Library/SuperStock; 11, © Pacific Stock/SuperStock; 13, © Robert Harding Picture Library/SuperStock; 14, © North Wind Picture Archives/Alamy; 15, © Hulton Archive/Getty Images; 16, © Lynette Cook/Photo Researchers, Inc.; 17, © Interfoto/Alamy; 18T, © Thomas & Pat Leeson/Photo Researchers, Inc.; 18B, Courtesy of United States Geological Survey; 19T, © SuperStock; 19B, © Larissa Jaster/iStockphoto; 20, © David Sanger/The Image Bank/Getty Images; 21T, © Corbis; 21B, Courtesy of Circus World Museum, Baraboo, Wisconsin; 22, Courtesy of United States Geological Survey; 23, © Jacques Langevin/Sygma/Corbis; 24, © Reuters/Corbis; 25, © Philippe Bourseiller/The Image Bank/Getty Images; 26, © John Cole/Photo Researchers, Inc.; 27, © John Cole/Photo Researchers, Inc.; 28, Courtesy of NASA/Johnson Space Center; 29, © Zach Holmes/Alamy; 31, © szefei/Shutterstock.

Publisher: Kenn Goin
Senior Editor: Lisa Wiseman
Creative Director: Spencer Brinker
Design: Dawn Beard Creative
Photo Researcher: Picture Perfect Professionals, LLC

Library of Congress Cataloging-in-Publication Data

Person, Stephen.
  Devastated by a volcano! / by Stephen Person.
     p. cm. — (Disaster survivors)
  Includes bibliographical references and index.
  ISBN-13: 978-1-936087-50-1 (library binding)
  ISBN-10: 1-936087-50-2 (library binding)
  1. Volcanoes—Juvenile literature. 2. Volcanologists—Juvenile literature. I. Title.
  QE521.3.P47 2010
  551.21—dc22
                              2009032630

For more information, write to Bearport Publishing Company, Inc., 101 Fifth Avenue, Suite 6R, New York, New York 10003. Printed in the United States of America in North Mankato, Minnesota.

112009
090309CGB

10 9 8 7 6 5 4 3 2 1

Contents

A Fiery Surprise

On June 25, 1997, Linda Daley was washing clothes outside her home on the Caribbean island of Montserrat (mont-suh-RAT). Just a few miles to the west rose the slopes of Soufrière (soo-free-AIR) Hills volcano. For the past 400 years, the volcano had been quiet. However, when Linda looked up from her work that day, she saw something shocking. Fiery clouds were shooting out of the mountain!

The island of Montserrat is only about 40 square miles (104 sq km)

"I felt this surge of heat and saw this great fire above me," Linda said. She dropped her bucket of water and ran away from the mountain. As the clouds came closer, she dove behind the wall of a nearby school building. "It got very dark, blacker than black," she said.

Fiery clouds shooting out of Soufrière Hills volcano

Scientists estimate that volcanoes have killed about 260,000 people in the past 300 years.

From Capital to Ghost Town

Linda hid behind the school until the wind blew the hot clouds away. Then she walked back to where she had been washing clothes. The metal bucket she had been using lay on the ground, totally melted. Other people on Montserrat were not as lucky as Linda. The volcano's **eruption** killed 19 people that day.

About 11,000 people lived on Montserrat before Soufrière Hills began erupting. Afterward, nearly 7,000 of them left the island in search of a safer place to live. Those who stayed moved to the "safe zone"—a part of the island believed to be out of reach of future eruptions.

The exclusion zone is the area where the people of Montserrat can no longer live.

Soufrière Hills erupted several more times in the following months. Each time, the volcano shot fiery, gray **ash** high into the air. The ash formed when hot liquid rock called **magma** exploded out of the volcano and quickly cooled. It hardened into pieces that were smaller than a grain of rice. By the end of 1997, Montserrat's capital city, Plymouth, was completely buried under ash.

As this picture shows, Plymouth is located dangerously close to Soufrière Hills.

These homes were covered in ash by the Soufrière Hills volcano eruption.

Why Do Volcanoes Erupt?

What caused the eruptions that nearly killed Linda and buried the city of Plymouth? The process began 60 miles (97 km) or more below Earth's surface. This deep underground, temperatures can reach over 2,500°F (1,371°C). It's so hot that the rock below Earth's surface can melt, turning into magma.

The rising magma often collects underground in a **magma chamber**. As gases bubble up inside the hot magma, the pressure within the chamber increases. This can force the magma to shoot up to Earth's surface.

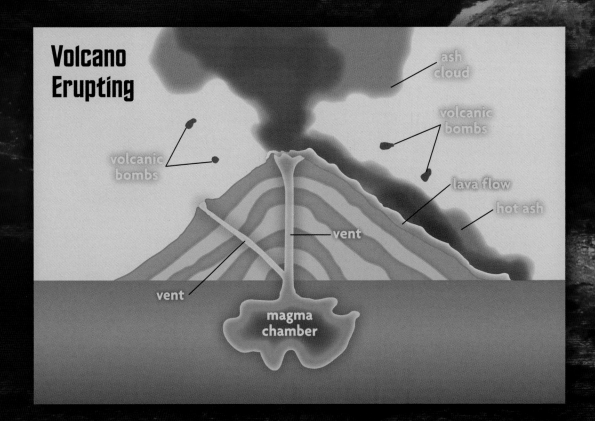

Volcano
Erupting

ash cloud

volcanic bombs

volcanic bombs

lava flow

hot ash

vent

vent

magma chamber

When magma reaches the surface, it comes out of an opening in the ground called a **vent**. It can burst out in an explosion of hot ash and pieces of flying rock called **bombs**, or more quietly as a **lava** flow.

A volcanic eruption in Hawaii

The color of lava depends on its temperature. At its hottest, it is usually bright orange. As it cools, it gets darker.

volcanic bombs

Mountains That Build Themselves

When a volcano erupts, lava flows, ash, and bombs collect around the volcano's vent. Over time, this material builds up around the vent in rocky layers. With each eruption, the layers of rock grow higher and higher, forming a volcanic mountain. This is why volcanoes are called "mountains that build themselves."

Entire mountains such as Mount Fuji in Japan have been formed by material from volcanic eruptions.

Some volcanoes, such as Mount Fuji in Japan, erupt thick lava that builds up into tall volcanic cones. Other volcanoes like Mount Kilauea (key-la-WAY-ah), an **active volcano** in Hawaii, erupt liquid lava that flows like a river down its sides. The lava can spread out over many miles. Then it cools and hardens into stone. This type of volcano grows to be very wide, but not very tall.

Though the lava that flows from Kilauea has destroyed nearly 200 homes on Hawaii, it moves slowly and is not usually dangerous to people.

Another volcano in Hawaii, Mauna Loa, rises nearly 11 miles (18 km) from its base on the sea floor to its peak 13,680 feet (4,170 m) above sea level. This makes Mauna Loa the largest volcano on Earth.

The Ring of Fire

Luckily for people, volcanoes are not found everywhere on Earth. They form mostly on the edges of **tectonic plates**, which are huge slabs of rock that cover Earth's surface. These plates move slowly, bumping into one another along their edges from time to time. When two plates collide, the edge of one plate can slide under the edge of the other. The sinking plate disturbs the rock below the surface, causing it to melt and form magma. This hot liquid then rises up to the surface, creating a volcano.

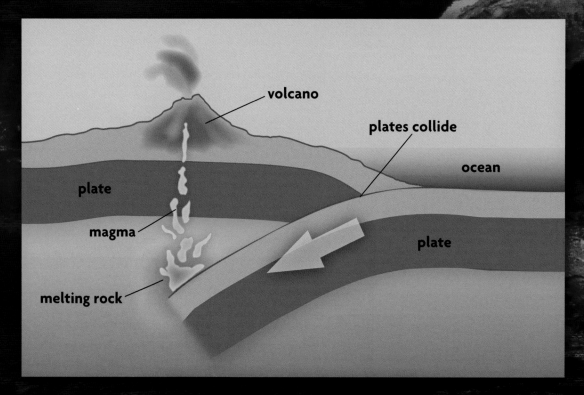

This diagram shows how the movement of tectonic plates can form a volcano.

More than half of the world's volcanoes are located above the edges of the plates that lie beneath the Pacific Ocean. This area has so many volcanoes that it's called the Ring of Fire.

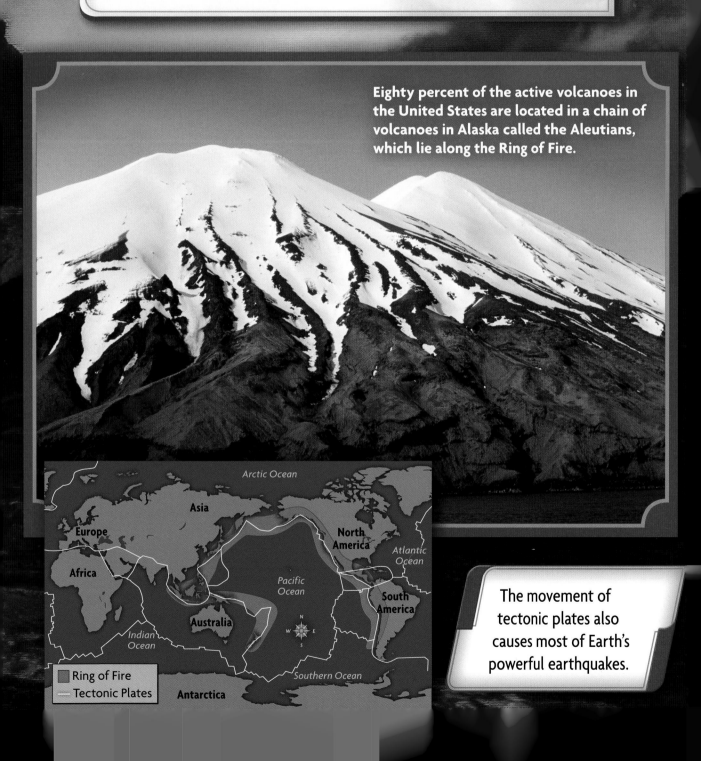

Eighty percent of the active volcanoes in the United States are located in a chain of volcanoes in Alaska called the Aleutians, which lie along the Ring of Fire.

The movement of tectonic plates also causes most of Earth's powerful earthquakes.

The Loudest Sound

One of the deadliest eruptions in history took place along the Ring of Fire in 1883. Krakatoa (krah-kuh-TOH-uh) was a **volcanic island** located in Indonesia. People thought that the volcano was **dormant** because it had been quiet for 200 years. However, this is not a long period of time in the life of a volcano.

Krakatoa before its famous eruption

On the morning of August 27, a British ship was sailing near Krakatoa. The crew heard a giant explosion. They saw the volcano blasting ash miles into the air, turning the sky black. Chunks of rock crashed down on the ship. Most frightening of all was the sound. The eruption was so loud that it was heard 3,000 miles (4,828 km) away!

Krakatoa erupting

Scientists think that the Krakatoa eruption may have been the loudest sound ever heard by humans.

Deadly Wall of Water

People on the nearby island of Java watched Krakatoa's eruption in horror. Then came an even more terrifying sight. The enormous blast pushed seawater away from the volcano. Giant waves called **tsunamis** formed and raced toward nearby islands. Some of the tsunamis were 135 feet (41 m) high—taller than a 10-story building!

As a tsunami hit Java, people ran toward higher ground. "The wave was too quick for most of them," said one farmer. "Many were drowned almost at my side." The eruption of Krakatoa killed about 36,000 people. Nearly all of them died in the tsunamis.

An eruption at Anak Krakatoa in June 2004

The force of the Krakatoa eruption caused the volcano to collapse into the sea. A new active volcano is rising in its place. The new volcano is called Anak Krakatoa, meaning "child of Krakatoa."

17

Mount St. Helens Blows Its Top

Scientists have learned a lot about volcanoes in the years since the eruption of Krakatoa. American **volcanologists** got a close-up look at a massive eruption in 1980. In March, steam began rising from Mount St. Helens in Washington State. When steam and hot gases rise from a volcano, scientists know that magma may be building up inside.

Mount St. Helens before the eruption in 1980

Volcanologist David Johnston at work near Mount St. Helens, just a day before the eruption

On the morning of May 18, volcanologist David Johnston was working just a few miles from Mount St. Helens. Suddenly, there was an explosion. The entire top of the mountain was blown into the sky. "This is it!" David shouted over his radio to other scientists. Sadly, it was the last message he ever sent.

Mount St. Helens blasted so much ash into the air that several inches of the gray powder fell in Montana, 500 miles (805 km) away.

After the eruption, Mount St. Helens was more than 1,300 feet (396 m) lower than it had been before.

The piece of the mountain that was blown away was as tall as the Empire State Building in New York City.

Killer Clouds

David was one of 57 people killed by Mount St. Helens. Like many large eruptions, this one created killer clouds called **pyroclastic flows**. These fast-moving clouds are made up of hot ash and **poisonous** gases. People caught in them can be burned badly or choked to death. Scientists believe that David was killed by a pyroclastic flow.

A pyroclastic flow speeds down the side of Soufrière Hills.

pyroclastic flow

When volcanoes kill large numbers of people, it is often because of pyroclastic flows. On the Caribbean island of Martinique, Mount Pelée erupted in 1902. A cloud of gas and ash sped toward the town of St. Pierre. Of the 28,000 people in the town, only two survived.

The eruption of Mount Pelée left the town of St. Pierre in ruins.

The pyroclastic flows from Mount Pelée moved 100 miles per hour (161 kpm), giving people in St. Pierre no chance to escape.

Louis-Auguste Cyparis survived Mount Pelée because he was locked alone in an underground prison. His survival story became famous, and he even toured with the Barnum & Bailey circus!

Tragedy in the Andes

Giant waves and deadly clouds are not the only ways volcanoes can kill. On November 13, 1985, Nevado del Ruiz (neh-VAH-doh DEL roo-EEZ) in Colombia erupted. The heat of the eruption melted snow and ice on the mountain. Water from the melted snow and ice mixed with volcanic ash and other **debris** to create a river of mud called a **lahar**. This river flowed down the mountain toward the town of Armero.

Nevado del Ruiz is a 17,500-foot (5,334-m) active volcano located in the Andes Mountains in Colombia, a country in South America.

A student named José ran into a hotel when he saw the lahar roaring into town. "It was a wall of mud," he said. "It crashed against the rear of the hotel and started crushing walls." José survived the lahar, though about 23,000 people were killed.

The town of Armero was destroyed by the lahar.

Nevado del Ruiz was the second deadliest eruption of the entire 20th century. Only the eruption of Mount Pelée in 1902 killed more people.

Volcanologists to the Rescue!

Volcanologists cannot **predict** exactly when volcanoes like Nevado del Ruiz will erupt. They can often tell when a volcano is becoming dangerous, however. In March 1991, several tiny earthquakes shook the ground near Mount Pinatubo (pee-na-TOO-boh) in the Philippines. Volcanologists raced to the area. They knew that earthquakes can be caused by magma rising inside a volcano.

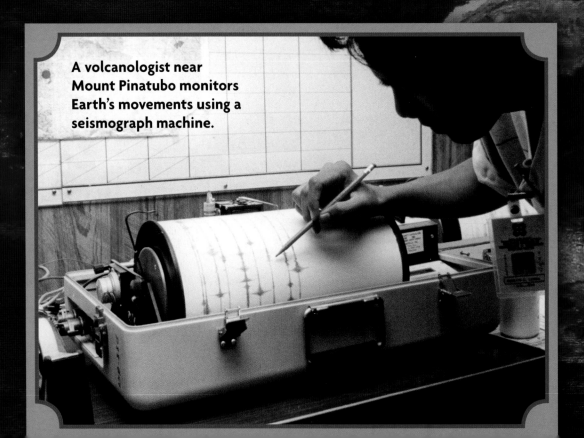

A volcanologist near Mount Pinatubo monitors Earth's movements using a seismograph machine.

In April and May, volcanologists detected more tiny earthquakes. They warned that a major eruption was possible. More than 60,000 people **evacuated** the nearby area. Sure enough, Mount Pinatubo erupted on June 15. Massive pyroclastic flows sped down the mountain. About 800 people were killed, but the scientists' warnings had saved thousands of lives.

People who lived near Mount Pinatubo evacuating the area

Mount Pinatubo blasted huge amounts of ash and volcanic gases into the air. The gas and ash blocked sunlight, causing Earth's average air temperature to cool nearly 1°F (.6°C) during the following year.

Digging Out

Volcanologists are hard at work on the island of Montserrat as well. Steam and hot gas still rise from Soufrière Hills. This gives scientists a great chance to study an active volcano up close. They will warn citizens if another major eruption seems likely.

About 4,000 survivors of the 1997 eruption are still living in the safe zone on Montserrat. They know the area around Soufrière Hills is dangerous. As soon as scientists say it is safe, however, they plan to dig out their capital city. "We won't give up so easy," said a storeowner named Nigel. "We'll carry on till we can come back to Plymouth."

The eruption of Soufrière Hills is not the first natural disaster to hit the people of Montserrat. Hurricane Hugo damaged most homes on the island in 1989.

Workers built a new airport on Montserrat in 2005. The old one was destroyed by the eruption of the Soufrière Hills volcano.

Famous Eruptions

Volcanoes can erupt at any time. Some cause more damage than others. Here are some of the most destructive and deadly volcanoes in history.

Mount Vesuvius, Italy, 79 A.D.

- The eruption of Mount Vesuvius buried the cities of Pompeii and Herculaneum under ash. More than 3,000 people were killed by the eruption.
- Pompeii and Herculaneum remained buried under ash for almost 1,700 years.
- Scientists have uncovered large parts of these towns. Today, they are popular tourist attractions.

Mount Unzen, Japan, 1792

- Eruptions of Mount Unzen caused landslides and tsunamis that killed more than 15,000 people.
- Mount Unzen erupted again in 1991. Pyroclastic flows killed 43 people.

Mount Tambora, Sumbawa Island, Indonesia, 1815

- A massive eruption created tsunamis and pyroclastic flows, killing about 10,000 people.
- Falling ash and volcanic gases, which caused the temperature to drop, ruined the crops of farmers on Sumbawa Island. More than 80,000 people died of starvation or disease.
- This is considered the deadliest volcanic eruption in recorded history.

Mount Tambora is still an active volcano.

Volcano Safety

Scientists offer the following advice for volcano safety:

- ☑ Stay away from erupting volcanoes.
- ☑ If you live near a volcano, make sure your family has an evacuation plan. Pick a place where your family will meet in case of an emergency, and plan how you will travel to safety.
- ☑ Keep your home stocked with the supplies that you will need in case of an eruption. These include a first-aid kit, a flashlight with extra batteries, a battery-operated radio, food and water, and goggles and masks to protect you and your family from falling ash.
- ☑ If you're stuck inside during an eruption, quickly close all the windows and doors. Close any other openings in the home that might allow ash to get inside.
- ☑ If you're stuck outside during an eruption, seek higher ground to avoid the danger of lahars or lava flows. Cover your mouth and nose with a mask or cloth.
- ☑ Use a radio and telephone to get the latest safety information.

Posted near Mount Rainier in Washington State, this sign points to the route to safety in case of an eruption.

Glossary

active volcano (AK-tiv vol-KAYN-oh) a volcano that has released gas and lava, even in small amounts, within the last 200 to 500 years

ash (ASH) tiny pieces of dust that are formed when magma explodes into the air and quickly cools and hardens

bombs (BOMZ) large pieces of magma that harden as they are thrown into the air by volcanoes

debris (duh-BREE) pieces of something that has been destroyed

dormant (DOR-muhnt) when a volcano has not erupted for a very long time, but could erupt again

eruption (i-RUP-shun) anytime fresh magma reaches Earth's surface and explodes in any form such as lava or ash

evacuated (i-VAK-yoo-ate-id) moved away from an area that is dangerous

lahar (la-HAR) a mudflow made of water and volcanic debris

lava (LAH-vuh) hot liquid rock that comes out of a volcano

magma (MAG-muh) hot liquid rock beneath the surface of Earth

magma chamber (MAG-muh CHAYM-bur) a place where magma pools up or collects beneath the surface

poisonous (POI-zuhn-us) when something is deadly

predict (pri-DIKT) to say what one thinks will happen in the future

pyroclastic flows (*pye*-roh-KLAS-tik FLOHZ) fast-moving clouds of hot ash and deadly gases, often part of volcanic eruptions

tectonic plates (tek-TAWN-ik PLAYTS) massive slabs of rock that make up Earth's surface

tsunamis (tsoo-NAH-meez) very destructive waves caused by a volcanic eruption or earthquake

vent (VENT) an opening through which liquid, steam, or gas can escape

volcanic island (vol-KAN-ik EYE-luhnd) the top of a volcano that rises out of the sea, forming an island

volcanologists (*vol*-kuhn-AH-loh-jists) scientists who study volcanoes

Bibliography

Larmer, Brook. "Another Paradise Lost." *Newsweek* (August 18, 1997).

Winchester, Simon. *Krakatoa: The Day the World Exploded.* New York: Harper Perennial (2003).

volcano.oregonstate.edu

www.geology.sdsu.edu/how_volcanoes_work

Read More

Berger, Melvin and Gilda. *Why Do Volcanoes Blow Their Tops?* New York: Scholastic (2000).

Fradin, Judy and Dennis. *Volcanoes: Witness to Disaster.* Washington, D.C.: National Geographic (2007).

Learn More Online

To learn more about volcanoes, visit
www.bearportpublishing.com/DisasterSurvivors

Index

About the Author

*Stephen Person has written many children's books
about the environment, nature, and history.
He lives with his family in Brooklyn, New York.*